Born In Babylon

My Road to Emmaus

By Jane M. Iery

TEACH Services, Inc.
P U B L I S H I N G
www.TEACHServices.com • (800) 367-1844

World rights reserved. This book or any portion thereof may not be copied or reproduced in any form or manner whatever, except as provided by law, without the written permission of the publisher, except by a reviewer who may quote brief passages in a review.

The author assumes full responsibility for the accuracy of all facts and quotations as cited in this book. The opinions expressed in this book are the author's personal views and interpretations, and do not necessarily reflect those of the publisher.

This book is provided with the understanding that the publisher is not engaged in giving spiritual, legal, medical, or other professional advice. If authoritative advice is needed, the reader should seek the counsel of a competent professional.

Copyright © 2022 Jane M. Iery
Copyright © 2022 TEACH Services, Inc.
ISBN-13: 978-1-4796-1433-2 (Paperback)
ISBN-13: 978-1-4796-1434-9 (ePub)
Library of Congress Control Number: 2022903323

Scripture quotations marked NJKV are taken from the New King James Version®. Copyright © 1982 by Thomas Nelson. Used by permission. All rights reserved.

Scripture quotations marked NIV are taken from THE HOLY BIBLE, NEW INTERNATIONAL VERSION®, NIV® Copyright © 1973, 1978, 1984, 2011 by Biblica, Inc.® Used by permission. All rights reserved worldwide.

Published by

Dedication

To those still in Babylon.

"And I heard another voice from heaven saying, 'Come out of her, my people, lest you share in her sins, and lest you receive of her plagues.'"
Revelation 18:4

Table of Contents

Special Acknowledgements............vii

1. The Journey Begins 9

2. Seeking Truth 19

3. The Seal of God 36

4. Antichrist Revealed 43

5. Wrong Pasture 61

6. Ezekiel's Role....................77

7. Mary, Queen of Heaven? 84

8. Becoming Adventist................91

Epilogue: Life as an Adventist 103

Bibliography 110

Special Acknowledgements

To those who have unconditionally supported me in my journey to the truth. To my dear sweet husband, Dan. I thank God every day for you. There are no words that can express what walking this path with you has meant to me. Not only growing more in love with each other, but better yet, growing more in love with God and His holy Word together. Our road has had its potholes, but with our eyes fixed on Jesus and Heaven as our goal, we can do nothing but overcome.

To my dearest friend Tom, a man of few words. You kept me breathing when the enemy tried to stifle me. Thank you, my friend.

To my sister in Christ, Carol. The day I said, "I think I have a book in me" is one I will never forget. Your simple reply of "I can't wait to read it" was a pivotal moment in the next three years of my life. I thank you for your encouragement.

To Brenda. There are no words that can express the thanks I have for God sending you into my life and for all your hard work editing my book. You have gone above and beyond the call.

To Pastor Aron Crews. Thank you for your faithfulness to God's holy Word and for answering His call.

And to God. For Your endless forgiveness, grace, love, and mercy. For saving me and trusting me to accomplish this task. All praise, honor, and glory belong only to You.

Chapter One

The Journey Begins

"Even there Your hand shall lead me, And Your right hand shall hold me" (Ps. 139:10).

I was born the fifth child out of seven into a large, beautiful family. Nieces, nephews, aunts, uncles, and a bazillion cousins filled my childhood with incredibly happy memories. Family gatherings were always times of joy, and I especially looked forward to the big ones! Christmas Eve was celebrated at *both* grandparents' homes, and our annual family reunion took place on the Fourth of July.

In fact, I thought the Fourth of July was named that because of our picnic. Yearly, relatives from everywhere would return to Uncle George's camp on Pike Lake for a feast of good food and even better company. This favorite family tradition began in 1933 with three couples (and a baby) deciding to celebrate our country's birthday, and attendance has grown to more than 200 people. Family is especially important to me.

I was raised in the Catholic tradition. Mom and Dad were very devout in their religious practice and raised us to be devout as well. We attended Mass every Sunday and were sure to be there on other days deemed "holy." All of us children were baptized by sprinkling as infants. I was nine days old when I was relieved of "original sin" and entered the Catholic Church. Godparents were chosen by my mom and dad to help me on my spiritual journey, although I do not ever remember them filling that role. But I still loved them and will always think of them fondly.

When I was going into the third grade, it became possible for our parents to send us all to the Catholic school in a neighboring city. The public school system was now allowing those who wished to attend the parochial school to ride their buses, so Mom and Dad jumped at the chance to have their children taught at church not only by the nuns and priests but also by schoolteachers with the same religious values. I loved school, and I loved being Catholic. I was a good student, and a few of my proudest moments were in sixth and seventh grades when I received the

"Religion" award. Mom was especially happy with me at the ceremony where I received the sacrament of confirmation. I was the first one to raise my hand and answer the first question the bishop of our diocese had asked. Of course, these questions were taken from our catechisms and were written in question-and-answer form. Growing up in my Catholic home meant learning and memorizing not Scripture but our catechism and many prayers. Prayers not only to God as in the form of the Lord's Prayer, but to Mary, Joseph, and a myriad of angels and saints. Although we had a Bible, God's Word was never read out loud to us, nor were we ever taught from it. One thing we did do and did very often, was say the rosary.

A rosary is a prayer aid that provides a physical method of keeping count of the number of Hail Mary's you have said, as the "mysteries" of Jesus' life are contemplated. The fingers are moved along the beads as the prayers are recited with ten beads (called a decade) for the Hail Mary, while the Lord's Prayer is said on the one large bead before each decade. There were five decades on each rosary, and each decade was assigned a mystery. In my early years, those included the Joyful, Glorious, and Sorrowful Mysteries. In 2002 Pope John Paul

II added the Luminous Mystery. Each set of mysteries were assigned to certain days of the week, and it was important to remember which mystery belonged to which day. My mother had a strong devotion to Mary, the mother of Jesus. It was common to find our family each evening kneeling around the furniture in our living room reciting the rosary. As a child, I never liked when Mom would announce that it was time to "say the rosary." My knees hurt, and I found the sheer repetition of the prayers quite boring. I would do a mental countdown of each decade, hoping the end would come quickly. Saying the rosary was not confined to the living room but was also recited in every family car ride that was going to take ten minutes or more, which is approximately the time it takes to complete the five decades.

When I was ten years old, tragedy hit our happy family. After graduating from high school, my oldest brother Johnny, age eighteen, was hired at the local iron ore mine, where he was killed in a freak accident. This devastated our family, and it was the first time I had ever witnessed my father crying. Johnny's funeral was attended by so many people and was a testimony to me of the love and respect my family had from our family, friends,

The Journey Begins

neighbors, and community. My brother was an exceedingly kind person and had even taught my parents the meaning of tithing. I knew he was in heaven with God and that if I were a good girl and a good Catholic, I would see him again someday.

In my teens, life started going down paths that would lead me to make many poor decisions. I believe this all started when I was unable to join extra-curricular activities at school. My oldest sister was a cheerleader, and I dreamed of following in her footsteps. Friday evenings consisted of going to the home basketball games to watch her cheer the team on. But living fourteen miles from the school presented challenges to get to required practices. Our family only had one vehicle, and with Dad working swing shifts, transportation to and from the school was sometimes not available. I did participate in cheerleading in sixth and seventh grades, but by the time I was in eighth grade, Mom had decided that I would not be able to join the cheerleading squad. It was just too difficult to get me back and forth and meet everyone's needs in the family. My oldest sister was able to complete high school with four years as a cheerleader only because other relatives that lived in our neighborhood were also involved and could make ride-sharing available.

I started smoking cigarettes at the age of thirteen and drinking beer at fifteen. It was not uncommon in the small neighborhood where I grew up. Like many others in our community, I personally did not come from a home where alcohol was readily available, and I rarely saw my parents drink. Both Mom and Dad were very hard-working people, and it just was not part of their lifestyle. In fact, the only times I can remember being around alcohol were at family events such as Christmas Eve, the Fourth of July picnic, or the occasional wedding reception. I do not ever recall seeing my dad drunk, although I do remember Mom being a little silly on two or three occasions. "We not only drink beer ... we bless it," stated a Catholic priest who was the guest speaker at a lecture I once attended. Alcohol was an acceptable part of a Catholic's life. After all, fermented wine was part of the weekly Sunday Mass.

So, why did I take to drinking? I believe it was out of boredom. There just was not a lot to do in our remote area, and even though my parents did not drink very often, some neighbors and relatives did. Weekends consisted of getting older cousins to purchase a six-pack of beer and a pack of cigarettes. Back then, a six-pack only cost $1.10, and both my best friend and I could become intoxicated very cheaply.

By the time I was old enough to legally buy my own alcohol at the age of eighteen, I had acquired a taste for it. I did not drink every day, but often enough. It was at this time that marijuana was also introduced into my life. Since it was not legal at the time and harder to obtain, my use of it was very sporadic. At this time, I also started my first real job as a waitress, bought my first car, and met the man who would become my first husband. And with these new privileges came the relief of not being obligated to say the rosary at home, a duty I did not miss.

> *Alcohol was an acceptable part of a Catholic's life. After all, fermented wine was part of the weekly Sunday Mass.*

Immediately after graduating from high school, I moved into my first apartment. Mom was not too keen on the idea and even stated that she knew I would be back home in a month or two. Within six months of living on my own, I found myself pregnant. Back then, marriage was the obvious option. So, I got married to a man I knew I did not love. One of my most vivid memories of the wedding ceremony is of walking down the aisle and thinking to myself, "I wonder how long this marriage will last." Not exactly how one wants their marriage to start out!

Drinking took a back seat as I began my journey as the young mother of my first son. Within two years, I had a daughter. Boredom was no longer an issue. Unfortunately, my marriage, a mistake from the beginning, was falling apart. Five years after we said, "I do," we were standing in a courtroom signing divorce papers.

During the separation phase from my husband, I began to visit bars with girlfriends after our shift ended at our waitressing job. It was in a bar that I met my next husband, and he liked to drink. *We* liked to drink. I fell head-over-heels in love with Dan, and only eighteen days after my divorce was finalized, we were married. Dan wanted children of his own, and so we decided to add to our family as soon as we could. During this time, my attendance in church was almost nonexistent. I was caught up in living in the world and enjoying what I could. This lasted until we moved to my hometown and lived close to Mom and Dad. Not wanting to be a disobedient daughter, I returned to the church of my childhood and even joined the choir. Very shortly after, I became pregnant with my third child, a son we named Paul.

Drinking was still a big part of our lives, and even though my husband and I both worked, we always seemed to struggle financially. Life was not always easy, and money was always short. Even though I continued to drink, I still faithfully attended church and always took my children with me, making sure they attended Sunday School and received their required sacraments of First Communion and Confirmation. Even if I was hungover, I was sure to attend Sunday Mass.

When my two oldest children were in their "tween" years, my ex-husband petitioned the court for custody and lost. I was pregnant with my fourth child at the time. A year later, he once again petitioned the court for custody. This time I was now expecting child number five, and under poor legal advice, I reluctantly gave up primary custody of my first two children. Once my youngest child was born, I began drinking more and more. Although

I did not recognize it at the time, depression had started to slowly overtake me. And yet life continued and changes I was not expecting started to happen.

Attending church began to have an influence on me. I began to desire spiritual matters and wished to participate more fully in the liturgy of the Mass. I had enjoyed singing in the choir but felt a need for more involvement. It did not take long before I became a lector (one who reads Scripture during Mass) and a Eucharistic Minister (one who assists the priest at communion time), offering the wine to participants. I especially enjoyed reading Scripture. Each lector was given a handbook to guide us in our preparation, and this handbook provided a little background to the biblical passages we would be reading. I looked forward to learning more about these stories and offered my services as lector as often as they would let me. God's Word would soon prove that "It shall not return to Me void" (Isa. 55:11).

Chapter Two

Seeking Truth

"I love those who love me, And those who seek me diligently will find me" (Prov. 8:17).

When my middle child, Paul, was about six years old, my two youngest were both still in diapers. One afternoon while I was busy attending to the little ones' needs, Paul, who was sitting in a rocking chair watching cartoons on television, asked me, "Mom, can you get me a drink of milk?"

My eyes glanced from my six-week-old lying on the sofa getting his messy diaper changed to the one-year-old sitting on the floor next to me, waiting his turn.

"Paul, you are not crippled; you can get your own drink," was my response.

"What's 'crippled,' Mom?" He was stalling.

"Well, you know how you see some people in wheelchairs?" By this time, I was getting a little perturbed. "And you know how some of those people can't do a whole lot for themselves? Well, Paul, you should be thanking God that you have two perfectly good legs. In fact, Paul, say 'Thank You, God, because I have two perfectly good legs.'"

My sweet little six-year-old boy repeated, "Thank You, God, because I have two perfectly good legs," then added, "but I'm still not getting the milk."

Isn't that how it goes sometimes with our spiritual journey? We know we have the "perfectly good legs," the means to keep on the path and grow in God's Word. I thought I had the resources to assist me on my journey to a closer relationship with my Lord and Savior. I had Bibles, several of them, in various translations. I had the Catechism of the Catholic Church (CCC), which was supposed to contain all the knowledge I would ever need to lead me to Christ and be a good Catholic. One of the teachings made an impact on me in the CCC. Section 2, Article V, 133 states: "Ignorance of the Scripture is ignorance of Christ" (https://1ref.us/1q2, accessed August 19, 2021). I certainly did not want to be ignorant and so began to pursue what was in the written Word of God.

Not really knowing how to go about doing that, I sought out Christian programming on the television. Early one morning, as my son Paul was eating breakfast before school, I was flipping through channels and came across a woman preaching the Word of God. It shocked me to see a woman standing on a stage in front of a very large audience, teaching from the Word. This would never have happened in a Catholic setting. I was intrigued and found her teaching relatable to my daily life. I liked her and even wanted to be like her. I wanted to be able to know the Word of God well enough to stand up and preach. Of course, being Catholic, I knew that was never going to happen, but I figured I could still learn. So, for the next few years, every morning at 6:30 a.m., Monday through Friday, I listened to this woman, Joyce Meyers.

In the fall of 1998, a program called Lay Ministry Leadership School was offered to parishioners in our diocese who were interested in ways to become leaders in their own faith community. Class size was limited, and applicants were required to go

> *I wanted to be able to know the Word of God well enough to stand up and preach.*

through an interview process. Both my mother and I were accepted into the program and became the very first mother/daughter team to attend the two-year course. I was thrilled at the possibility of getting to know my Lord and Savior on a personal level.

One weekend a month for two years, we studied and learned how to lead a more well-rounded Catholic life. The classes taught me a great deal on many subjects that would be helpful in parish life. My own parish was seeking to fill the position of pastoral associate and taking these courses only aided in my subsequent nineteen-year ministry in that role. Unfortunately, Scripture did not play a big role in that part of my education. Upon completing the course, I was ordained a lay minister. But still, I felt something was missing, and I longed for more. What I was hungry for was knowledge contained in the written Word.

Along with my duties as the new pastoral associate of my parish came opportunities to initiate programs for members of my church. I repeated my son's milk story in front of my congregation while promoting a Bible study group I was attempting to organize for the women of the church. I followed up by placing an announcement in the weekly bulletin, handed out flyers to encourage participation, and finally placed a signup sheet in a prominent place in the entry of our church so that all would have easy access to it. I did not want anyone to miss out. Imagine my surprise when fourteen women showed up for the first class. I was thrilled and could not wait to share and grow in God's Word. We each had our "Little Rock Bible" study guide in hand and were eager to delve into territory unknown. The Catholics of my acquaintance were not known for their biblical knowledge, and I wanted to change that. Unfortunately, we were a group with no Bible teacher to lead us, and it became apparent that we were out of our element. By the time the program ended six weeks later, the group had dwindled to four women. Repeated attempts to hold Bible study groups resulted in those same four participants struggling to understand sacred Scripture. Each of these lessons contained what I consider to be "fluff" teachings, the pretty stuff on top. For me, there was no depth, and my hunger for the truth only deepened.

As my pastoral duties continued, I remained active in pursuing any learning opportunities that my diocese would periodically offer. It was while attending one of those events that

I was introduced to LIMEX. An extension program from the Loyola Institute for Ministry was coming to the city of Marquette, only a twenty-five-minute drive from my house. It was a four-year course, and my parish was willing to pay the tuition. The cost of the books would be my responsibility, which I cheerfully accepted. Soon my weekly classes began. For three hours every Tuesday evening, I would set aside the rest of the world to learn more about God. I was all in, knowing my spiritual life was going to take me into a personal relationship with the Creator of our universe.

I even bought a new Bible! It was the required Catholic Study Bible, and it came with a hefty price tag. I did not care because finally, I was going to have the chance to study with other starving students. Unfortunately, the new Bible I had purchased was rarely used. One would think that a theology class would teach some theology. In those four years, I learned an enormous amount of incredibly good things, good Catholic things, but again I was left unsatisfied with no real grasp of the Bible. Except this time, little gospel seeds were being planted.

Those seeds were coming not from any of the classes I was taking but from the lessons

I was hearing on my car radio while commuting to class every Tuesday night. To get to class, I needed to drive those twenty-five miles, and it just so happened that on the local Christian radio station Dr. David Jeremiah had a Bible study program that aired during my time behind the wheel. I was not used to hearing this type of preaching, and it grabbed me. The Old Testament was shedding light on the New Testament. It was not just the feel-good stuff that tickled your ears. I longed to hear more and soon discovered similar Bible programs on that station with preachers such as Erwin Lutzer, Alister Begg, and Charles Swindoll, to name a few. God's Word began to grow in me, and I eventually bought a radio for home. With all my children grown and out of the house, I had turned one of their bedrooms into my personal prayer room, a place where I could pray and listen to "my programs." These half-hour glimpses into the Bible became part of an important routine for me. I began to understand the importance of the Old Testament, how it connects, completes, and makes sense out of the New Testament.

Even though I was grateful for my programs, I continued to seek ways to grow spiritually, especially if it involved God's Word.

Though I was already being spiritually fed, if another opportunity came up, I took advantage of it, especially if there was no cost attached.

Anyone looking at me would think I was a model Catholic. Most of my family had no idea about the degree of my alcoholism, but, of course, neither did I. As time went on, my marriage to Dan was slowly crumbling. There was no way I was getting another divorce, so maintaining the appearance of a good marriage was important. But this only added to my depression. And then came the anxiety and panic attacks. These attacks would start with me feeling a little nervous and then would escalate to an uncontrollable heart-pounding and feverish shaking of my body. My worst attack happened one day while I was reading Scripture at the podium during Sunday Mass. I fainted and was assisted by two church members who happened to be first responders for the local fire department. I discovered that one way to help control a panic attack was to have a shot of liquor. Satan had a total grip on me. He was also working on my husband. When I look back at those days, I truly believe that the closer I got to God's truth, the worse my alcoholism became. Satan knew that if I discovered what was in the Word, he would lose one more soul. And Satan does not like to lose.

My husband's alcoholism was also escalating, and although sharing the same address, we were no longer living as a married couple. Evenings at home found me sitting at the end of the couch with a vodka bottle within arm's reach. Dan chose to be either in a bar or camping miles away.

At this time, I was also working a full-time job, and my consumption of alcohol became a daily habit. Drinking straight vodka on my lunchtime became routine and started affecting my performance on the job. A co-worker noticed, and now my job was on the line.

Being Catholic, I decided to seek help from a social service organization owned by the mother church, and it was there that I was assigned to be counseled by a man named Tom. I later discovered that he himself had suffered from depression and was a recovering alcoholic, reasons why he had become a therapist specializing in those areas.

Here is where God's blessing began. Within a few sessions, the road to healing was being paved. Tom suggested I see my doctor and get something for the depression. He explained to me that with the amount of alcohol I was consuming, the wiring in my brain was being affected. Antidepressants could help "rewire" it. I was determined to make this work, and so I did as he suggested and immediately made an appointment to see my doctor.

Tom also told me that one of the side effects of the antidepressant was its ineffectiveness when mixed with alcohol. I quit drinking the day I began taking the antidepressants, and to this day, God has totally relieved me of the urge to drink. With help, my panic attacks were also under control, and the healing was beginning, and it was happening fast, a lot faster than I could ever have imagined.

But Satan was not giving up. That "help" was marijuana. I had used it periodically throughout my adult life and had a fondness for it. It soon became my drug of choice to ease the anxiety. It made a difference, and it was legal in my state for medical purposes. I obtained my medical marijuana card and quickly found a caretaker (one who grows and sells marijuana). With the antidepressants and the marijuana, I felt the best I had ever felt in twenty years. I continued my therapy, and my marriage started to come back into place.

Seeking Truth

Dan's path to recovery began very shortly after mine. One month after I quit drinking, he also became sober. God now began putting *us* back together. It did not happen overnight, but it happened. Satan was not pleased with this and often tried to put a wedge between us. Even today, if Dan and I are not watchful, the enemy will do his best to place annoyances in our minds. He takes pleasure in trying to destroy what God created in His image, "…in the image of God He created him; male and female He created them" (Gen. 1:27). The destruction of marriages and families is one of Satan's goals, for it is there he attempts to destroy the beautiful image of God.

My therapy with Tom lasted three years. Each year he would give me a black rubber wrist band with the word "warrior" on it. These three bands each represented the afflictions that had gripped me for so many years: depression, anxiety, and alcoholism. I wore these bands proudly, as they had become a symbol of the extremely hard work I had accomplished to get sober and mentally stable. Life was beginning to be fun again. My job was intact, and my marriage was on the mend. What more would our good Lord have in store for me? I was soon to find out.

> *Life was beginning to be fun again. My job was intact, and my marriage was on the mend. What more would our good Lord have in store for me?*

Arriving home from work one evening, I noticed a flyer on Dan's music stand. The evangelistic series *Unlock Revelation* was coming to the campus of Northern Michigan University in Marquette. Dan informed me that it had arrived in the mail and, as he handed it to me, he asked if I wanted to go. At that time, my husband, although incredibly supportive of me on my journey, did not attend church. For him to ask if I wanted to go *with* him prompted a big "yes" from me. The flyer stated that if we signed up online, we would receive a free DVD on the "Daniel Chronicles," so we registered. The flyer did not give the name of the church denomination affiliated with the event, so out of curiosity, I decided to do a little online investigating. I was able to find the originators of the flyer and discovered that the Seventh-day Adventist Church was sponsoring the event. After listening to so many different Protestant preachers, by this time, I did not really care which church it was. I was hungry and didn't care who fed me. I knew that if it were too far out in left field or if I didn't feel comfortable being there, I would not return. I at least wanted to give them a chance. Little did I know that my life was about to change in ways I never would have imagined.

Upon arriving at the university where the series was being held, we discovered that Bibles were made available to those who did not bring one with them. It had not even occurred to me to take mine, as it is not generally a practice for Catholics to carry a Bible to such events. I also decided that as long as free Internet was provided, I may as well attempt to download a Bible app on my new smartphone. Sure enough, a few minutes later, before class had even started, I had my first Bible application. I still have that app, along with several more, and continue to use it to this day.

The *Unlock Revelation* lessons started with the book of Daniel and were being presented by a very young man. Pastor Aron Crews was twenty-three years old, fresh out of college, and it soon became evident that he had a clear understanding of Scripture. One of the first things he impressed on all of us attending was that the lessons we were about to hear would come from the Word of God, not from himself. He explained, "Not because Pastor Aron says so, but because of what the Bible says. The Bible unlocks itself. Let the Bible interpret the Bible." He even quoted Scripture to back up this statement: "For precept must be upon precept, precept upon precept, Line upon line, line upon line, Here a little, there a little" (Isa. 28:10).

Pastor Crews went on to say that if one wants to understand the book of Revelation, it is imperative that the book of Daniel is also understood. Both were important as apocalyptic prophecies, and through diligent study, we (yes, even me) could begin to grasp their meaning. I would now, through God's Word, learn about the "beasts," the little horn, the mark of the beast, what the numbers 666 mean, and even who the antichrist points to.

Pastor Crews began explaining the events surrounding King Nebuchadnezzar's dream in Daniel 2:31–33. "You, O King, were watching; and behold, a great image! This great image, whose splendor was excellent, stood before you; and its form was awesome. This image's head was of fine gold, its chest and arms of silver, its belly and thighs of bronze, its legs of iron, its feet partly of iron and partly of clay." He showed us how this statue represented the rise and fall of kingdoms and how this dream told of events that would make it into the history books. The head of gold was the rule of Babylon from 605–539 B.C. Next came chest and arms of silver belonging to the Medo-Persia era from 539–331 B.C. This kingdom was followed by the belly and thighs of brass pertaining to Greece, which reigned from 331–168 B.C. Rome was next with the legs of iron ruling from 168 B.C.–A.D. 476. After this came divided Rome depicted in the ten toes, completing the form of the image. I was fascinated. Many of these prophecies have already happened and can be proven in our history books. I was hooked. I was now very anxious for more.

This was just the beginning of my journey with Daniel. According to Daniel seven, God gives him a vision depicting the same time period but using different symbols. This time each kingdom is symbolized by animals or beasts. We learned in Daniel 7:17 that these beasts simply mean kings or kingdoms: "Those great beasts, which are four, are four kings, which arise out of the earth." The "head of gold" was now a lion with wings, representing Babylon's supreme reign on earth. Rather than the statue's chest and arms of silver, Medo-Persia was now a bear with three ribs in its mouth. Instead of the belly and thighs of brass, Greece was now a four-headed leopard with four wings. Alexander the Great ruled this kingdom until he died, at which time his empire was divided among his four top generals. A fierce beast with iron teeth and ten horns replaced the legs of iron, representing Rome's reign. The ten toes of the statue were now the ten horns of this beast, representing the division of the kingdom, which division still exists today. These beasts, we learned, show up again in the *book* of Revelation. I decided that there were no forces on earth that were going to prevent me from attending future classes. My only problem was that the *Unlock Revelation* series was four weeks long with a total of twenty-one lessons, not the four nights I mistakenly thought it would take. This part of the study of Daniel was just a prelude to what was to come, and I would have to wait a few sessions to learn the true unavoidable identity of the antichrist.

Unable to make a commitment to attend all the sessions, I was very delighted when they informed me that they were being videotaped and would become available online later. Each week I eagerly waited for the opportunity to sit in the comfort of my prayer room, alone, and continue studying the Revelation of our Lord Jesus Christ as seen through the eyes of His beloved apostle, John. Each week I gained knowledge of what God's Word was really saying. Each week Satan's lies were being unveiled, and the scales that were covering my eyes were being removed.

> *Each week I gained knowledge of what God's Word was really saying. Each week Satan's lies were being unveiled, and the scales that were covering my eyes were being removed.*

I was not prepared for the spiritual roller coaster ride I was about to embark upon.

Chapter Three

The Seal of God

"Moreover I also gave them My Sabbaths, to be a sign between them and Me, that they might know that I am the Lord who sanctifies them" (Ezek. 20:12).

The part of my spiritual journey that made a powerful impact on me was the lesson on the Sabbath, "The Day that Disappeared." As Catholics, we were taught to "Keep holy the Lord's Day" and that it was considered a "mortal" sin to miss Mass unless you were ill or traveling and it was impossible to get to a church. I was now learning that nowhere in the Bible did God change the Sabbath law and that it was the only commandment that began with the word "Remember." "Remember the Sabbath day, to keep it holy" (Exod. 20:8).

In Exodus 31:18, "He gave Moses two tablets of the Testimony, tablets of stone, written with the finger of God." Of stone ... with the **finger of God**? I knew the Ten Commandments had been written on stone, but I had never realized that they were written with the finger of God. Most of us have heard that when something is written in stone, it cannot be changed. To find out that it was with God's very finger made it much more important and worth paying attention to.

Pastor Crews explained that the Sabbath and Saturday are the same day. God was very explicit that the Sabbath is on the seventh day. "And on the seventh day God ended His work which He had done, and He rested on the seventh day from all His work which He had done. Then God blessed the seventh day and sanctified it ..." (Gen. 2:2–3). The word "the" used here is a definite article and is repeated three times, telling me it was important to remember.

He continued by reminding us that Jesus was crucified on Friday, "That day was the Preparation, and the Sabbath drew near" (Luke 23:54). The Sabbath falls on the day after "Preparation" day. No one can argue that the Christian world commemorates the crucifixion of Jesus on Good Friday. Not only has the whole Jewish nation kept the Sabbath on Saturday for millennia, but in 108 languages of the world, the word for the seventh day of the week is "Sabbath."

More insights brought out the fact that Jesus Himself kept the Sabbath. "And as His custom was, He went into the synagogue on the Sabbath day, and stood up to read" (Luke 4:16). And He expected that it would be kept in the future since He warned His followers concerning the destruction of the temple that would happen in 70 AD, some forty years after His resurrection. "And pray that your flight may not be in winter or on the Sabbath" (Matt. 24:20). Scripture shows us in Acts 17:2 that even Paul kept the Sabbath. "Then Paul, as his custom was, went into the synagogue, and for three Sabbaths reasoned with them from the Scriptures" (NIV).

Verse after verse points to Saturday as the day God set aside for us to keep holy, not Sunday. "And call the Sabbath a delight, the holy day of the Lord" (Isa. 58:13). "For the Son of Man is Lord even of the Sabbath" (Matt. 12:8). These verses are not what you will hear from the pulpit of a Catholic Church. The verse that clinched the Sabbath law for me came from the book of Isaiah, which shows that we will be coming together to worship God on the New Earth again on the day He sanctified and made holy. "'For as the new heavens and the new earth Which I will make shall remain before Me,' says the Lord, 'So shall your descendants and your name remain. And it shall come to pass That from one New Moon to another, and from one Sabbath to another, all flesh shall come to worship before me,' says the Lord" (Isa. 66:22–23).

Many Sunday keepers will argue that the apostles themselves came together, broke bread, and took up a collection on the first day of the week, stating their claim for Sunday services. They will point to verses such as 1 Corinthians 16:1–2 where Paul wrote: "Now concerning the collection for the saints, as I have given orders to the churches of Galatia, so you must do also: On the first day of the week let each one of you lay something aside, storing up as he may prosper, that there be no collections when I come. And when I come, whomever you approve by your letters I will send to bear your gift to Jerusalem." It is assumed that an assembly was held and a collection plate passed. Actually, Paul had sent a letter to the churches in Asia Minor, which would have been read to the believers on the Sabbath, saying to them that when they leave Sabbath worship and go home, not to forget to lay something aside on the next day, which would be the first day of the week or Sunday. (The Greek connotation here for "lay something aside" is to lay something aside *at your home*). Also, "storing up as he may prosper" can lead one to understand that if the believers were blessed in some way during the week, they were to share in that abundance.

Another verse which Sunday keepers use to prove the first-day theory is contained in Acts 20:7–8, which says: "Now on the first day of the week, when the disciples came together to break bread, Paul, ready to depart the next day, spoke to them and continued his message until midnight. There were many lamps in the upper room where they were gathered together." The argument tends to go like this: See? They came together on the first day and broke bread. But the breaking of bread simply meant that they had a meal together. They broke bread "daily" in Acts 2:46. "So continuing daily with one accord in the temple, and breaking bread from house to house, they ate their food with gladness and simplicity of heart."

"On the first day" and "there were many lamps" give us another clue to the day of their gathering. In Jewish culture the day began at evening. Leviticus 23:32 explains, "It shall be unto you a sabbath of solemn rest, ... from evening to evening, you shall celebrate your sabbath." Mark 1:32 says, "At evening when the sun had set, they brought unto Him all that were sick and those who were demon-possessed." It would have been against Jewish law to heal on the Sabbath, so people waited until it was over to bring their sick to Jesus.

"There were many lamps" shows that it had become dark outside and that Paul's Sabbath preaching had taken them into the evening, the first day of the week. Paul had stayed a full seven days to be with the people over the Sabbath. On Sunday morning, he and his companions walked twenty miles to join the boat at Assos. According to the commandment, they never would have participated in such secular activities on the Sabbath but would have done so on the first day of the week.

> *I would soon learn that the seal of God was also contained in the fourth commandment.*

I would soon learn that the seal of God was also contained in the fourth commandment. A seal is what makes a document official, and it normally contains three characteristics: name, office or title, and territory. An example can be found in Ezra 1:1. "Cyrus king of Persia." When Jesus was buried in the tomb, it was sealed by Pontius Pilate, governor of Judea, another example. At the end of the fourth commandment, it states: "For in six days the Lord [name] made [title as Creator] the heavens and the earth [territory]." This clearly gives us evidence that this commandment has God's seal placed in it.

The next thing I learned came from the prophetic books of Daniel and Revelation. As my eyes of understanding began to open, my spiritual world began to unravel. The roller coaster was picking up speed.

Chapter Four

Antichrist Revealed

"Blessed is he who reads and those who hear the words of this prophecy, and keep those things which are written in it; for the time is near" (Rev. 1:3).

Many years ago, I had read the verse quoted above and wanted that blessing. In one sitting I had devoured the whole book of Revelation. But my lack of guidance and understanding of this prophetic letter only left me confused and unsatisfied. Little did I know that those blessings would appear; they just would not be manifested in a way I could ever have imagined. My weekly appointment with the *Unlock Revelation* videos continued and was about to take an unexpected turn. As more studies unfolded, my faith in the accuracy of God's Word increased. And even though I looked forward to learning the truth, I had an uneasy feeling that things were about to change. That time of change would begin now as I delved into the video titled "The Unavoidable Identity of the Antichrist." This is the one I had been waiting for, and this is the one that would change my life forever.

In this *Unlock Revelation* session, Pastor Crews proposed that everyone attending would, without a shadow of a doubt, come to understand for themselves who the antichrist was by the evidence he was about to present. It would not be his own opinion, and he was confident it would become the consensus of all those who were present. At that time, I really wanted to skip to the end of the video but knew that he would use biblical texts to prove his case. If I was going to be a diligent student of the Bible, I needed to know for myself what that proof was. He eased us into it.

"Let no one deceive you by any means; for that Day will not come unless the falling away comes first, and the man of sin is revealed, the son of perdition" (2 Thess. 2:3). "That day" pertains to the second coming of Jesus, and apparently, it would be Christ's own followers that were going to have some kind of "falling away" (in Greek the word refers to apostasy or divorce). During the series, I had come to learn that Jesus recognizes His true church as a pure woman, and our reign with Him in heaven was symbolized as a marriage. We find this in Scripture: "I have likened the daughter of Zion To a lovely and delicate woman" (Jer. 6:2). "Let us be glad and rejoice and give Him glory, for the marriage of the Lamb has come, and His wife has made herself ready. And to her it was granted to be arrayed in fine linen, clean and bright, for the fine linen is the righteous acts of the saints" (Rev. 19:7–8). I had been divorced and knew firsthand the pain that can accompany it. I wondered how this "marriage" would be dissolved.

Paul tells us, "For I know this, that after my departure savage wolves will come in among you, not sparing the flock. Also from **among yourselves** men will rise up, speaking perverse things, to draw away the disciples after themselves" (Acts 20:29–30). This "falling away" was going to begin with the followers of Jesus Christ Himself. I was intrigued and even more anxious to see this video to the end.

In *Strong's Exhaustive Concordance*, on page 473, the word "anti" has these definitions:

a. instead of, in place of, because of, in the room of
b. Often used in composition to denote contrast, requital, substitution, correspondence, etc.

According to these definitions, the word "antichrist" then is not someone directly opposed to God. Instead, it is a person or a system that seeks to take the place of God. It is Satan who wants that worship for himself. "For you have said in your heart: 'I will ascend into heaven, I will exalt my throne above the stars of God; I will also sit on the mount of the congregation on the farthest sides of the north; I will ascend above the heights of the clouds, I will be like the Most High'" (Isa. 14:13–14). Satan himself substitutes, usurps, sneaks in as a replacement to Christ. But how does he do this and what will it look like?

The Bible provides eleven ways to identify this antichrist.

1. It arises out of pagan Rome, has Roman roots. (Dan. 7:8)
2. It has a prominent man at its head who speaks for it. (Dan. 7:8)
3. It comes up after the ten kingdoms are set. (Dan. 7:8)
4. It arises in Europe from among the divided kingdoms. (Dan. 7:8, 24)
5. It destroys three of the other horns/kingdoms, uprooting them. (Dan. 7:8)
6. It is a little kingdom. (Dan. 7:8)

7. It is different from the other kingdoms in that it is a religio-political power. (Dan. 7:24)
8. It reigns for 1,260 literal years. (Dan. 7:25)
9. It would intend to change God's times and laws. (Dan. 7:25)
10. It persecutes God's true people during its 1,260-year reign. (Dan. 7:25)
11. It speaks blasphemy, claiming divine authority. (Dan. 7:8, 25)

Pastor Crews asked us, "Have we been true to the biblical text? I propose that the antichrist is the Roman Church-State church, the historic Christian church, the medieval Christian church; the church that was married to God itself became the antichrist!"

> *The word "antichrist" then is not someone directly opposed to God. Instead, it is a person or a system that seeks to take the place of God.*

After hearing and seeing this, I paused the video. My mind was screaming, *how can this be? How can this be? This cannot be so!* I began to cry, and my entire body trembled uncontrollably. What was I going to do?

I knew from the many weeks of watching these videos that Pastor Crews would use biblical and historic evidence to explain his reasoning. I already knew in my heart that from what had been presented so far, this was all true. I restarted the video and tried to absorb the rest of the presentation.

Pastor Crews went on to explain each item on the list: First, in Daniel 7:8, it says that it began as a little horn (or kingdom). No one can argue that the smallest kingdom (horn) on the planet is the Vatican, the home of the papacy.

Second, we learned that it arose out of pagan Rome and had Roman roots (Dan. 7:24). In *Stanley's History*, p. 40, it states, "The popes filled the place of the vacant emperors of Rome, inheriting their power, prestige, and titles from paganism. The papacy is but the ghost of the deceased Roman Empire, sitting crowned upon its grave." _It came to power after A.D. 476.

Third, in Daniel 7:8, we find that the little horn "plucked out by the roots" the first three horns. In A.D. 476, when the Roman Empire ended, a struggle began for control of the ten parts of the empire. On one side were three of the pagan tribes: the Heruli, the Vandals,

Antichrist Revealed 49

and the Ostrogoths. On the other side were the Bishop of Rome and the emperors loyal to the Catholic bishop. One by one, the Catholic emperors overthrew these three rebel tribes:

- Emperor Zeno conquered the Heruli by encouraging the Ostrogoths
- to invade in A.D. 493.
- Emperor Justinian sent his General Belisarius to conquer the
- Vandals in A.D. 534.
- General Belisarius then drove the Ostrogoths out of Rome in A.D. 538.

In A.D. 533, Justinian had decreed that the Bishop of Rome was to rule supreme over all the churches. But this decree would mean nothing until he and other emperors overthrew the rebel tribes.

The fourth fact is the one that provoked tremendous anger in my heart toward my church for many days. I have asked God to forgive me and am incredibly grateful we have a loving and merciful Father. Daniel 7:8 says: "And there, in this horn, were eyes like the eyes of a man, and a mouth speaking pompous words." Revelation 13:1 uses the phrase "and on his heads a *blasphemous* name." The biblical definition of blasphemy can be found in Scripture itself: the **claim to be God** (see John 10:33) and **claiming to be able to forgive sins** (see Mark 2:7). So, does the Catholic Church make these bold statements? And if so, where in history will we find these claims? In the *Catholic National*, July 1895, Pope Pius X, while he was Archbishop of Venice, is quoted as saying: "The pope is not only the representative of Jesus Christ, but he is Jesus Christ Himself, hidden under the veil of the flesh. Does the pope speak? It is Jesus Christ who speaks. So that when the pope speaks, we have no business to examine" (Amazing Discoveries, https://1ref.us/1q7, accessed October 13, 2021). From the *Great Encyclical Letters of Leo XIII*, p. 304: "We hold upon this earth the place of God Almighty."

What? How could this be true? Surely there was some mistake. I could not believe what I was hearing and soon discovered that these are just a few examples. There are many more statements containing the same arrogance. My heart sank. Up to this time in my life, I had had a lot of respect for the office of the papacy. I could barely digest what I was hearing, and yet, there was still more waiting for me. Could this get any worse?

The second evidence of blasphemy concerned the forgiveness of sins. To be forgiven of our sins, Catholics are taught that they need to go confess to a priest. This was not a practice I participated in very often. Mostly, I went to confession when a family member was also present at a Catholic function where confessions were made. I didn't want to appear unholy.

In the publication *Dignities and Duties of the Priest*, vol. 12, p. 27, it states: "God Himself is obliged to abide by the judgment of His priests, and either not to pardon or to pardon, according as they refuse or give absolution ... The sentence of the priest precedes, and God **subscribes to it.**" Again, I was dumbfounded. God subscribes to it? The God who made the heaven and earth subscribes to mere man? *Joseph Deharbe's Catechism*, p. 279, states: "The priest does really and truly forgive sins in virtue of the power given to him by Christ." My faith in the Catholic Church was now being reduced to contempt, a contempt I had to, with the help of the Almighty Father, push aside. What more was this series going to teach me, and would I be able to bear it?

The lesson moved on with more "unavoidable" identifiers. I sat in my prayer room, holding my breath, waiting for whatever else was to come. I wasn't even sure how to feel anymore. Daniel 7:25 proceeds to say that this antichrist "shall persecute the saints of the Most High, And shall intend to change times and law. Then the saints shall be given into his hand For a time and times and half a time." A parallel verse in Revelation 13:5–7 says: "And he was given a mouth speaking great things and blasphemies, and he was given authority to continue for forty-two months. ... It was granted to him to make war with the saints and to overcome them." I wondered what "a time and times and half a time" and "forty-two months" could really mean.

> *I sat in my prayer room, holding my breath, waiting for whatever else was to come.*

These time periods are used in several places in Scripture and are also presented as 1,260 days (see Revelation 11:3 and 12:6). Parts of the book of Daniel and Revelation are written prophetically, and it is necessary to understand what certain symbols mean. Using the Bible to explain the Bible, we can find the formula for these time periods. In Ezekiel 4:6, we find that a day is equal to a year in prophecy. "I have laid on you a day for a year," and also in Numbers 14:34, "According to the number of the days in which you spied out the land, forty days, for each day you shall bear your guilt one year." In Jewish history a "time" is equal to one year; therefore, times is two years, and half a time would then be half a year, making a total of 1,260 days or 42 months or 3 ½ years.

"Then the saints shall be persecuted" points to the period in time when the Roman church-state reigned, otherwise known as the "Dark Ages." This power became supreme in Christendom in A.D. 538 due to a letter of the Roman emperor Justinian, known as Justinian's decree. This decree set up and acknowledged the bishop of Rome as the head of all churches. It gave the Roman church-state political power, civil power, as well as ecclesiastical power. It became part of Justinian's code, the fundamental law of the empire. That year, Pope Vigilius ascended the throne under the military protection of Belisarius (*The History of the Christian Church* – vol. 3, p. 327). The legally recognized supremacy of the pope was given full use of the state to enforce the Church's teachings. The papacy does not deny this: "It is therefore, by a particular decree of Divine Providence that, at the fall of the Roman empire and its partition into separate kingdoms, the Roman Pontiff, whom Christ made the head and center of his entire Church, acquired civil power" (Pope Pius IX, apostolic letter *Cum Catholica Ecclesia*, March 26, 1860).

In 1798, exactly 1,260 years later, the murder of a Frenchman in Rome gave the French an excuse for occupying the Eternal City and putting an end to papal temporal power. The aged pontiff himself was carried off into exile to Valence, France. The enemies of the Church rejoiced. The last pope, they declared, had reigned (*Church History*, p. 24). Berthier entered Rome on the tenth of February, 1798, and proclaimed a republic. Half of Europe thought Napoleon's veto would be obeyed and that with the capture of the pope, the papacy was dead (*The Modern Papacy*, Reverend Joseph Rickaby, p. 1). "That the Roman church-state has shed more innocent blood than any other institution that has ever existed among mankind will be questioned by no Protestant who has a competent knowledge of history." (*History of the Rise and Influence of Rationalism in Europe*, W.E.H. Lecky, Vol. 2,

p. 32). According to *Public Ecclesiastical Law*, vol. 2, p. 142, "The church may by divine right confiscate the property of heretics, imprison their persons and condemn them to the flames" ("Roman Catholic Ten Commandments"). During its 1,260-year reign, papal persecutions brought death to millions. As a young student, I had heard of the Dark Ages but had never understood the true meaning or ramifications of it. My heart ached. My head ached. My body ached for these true saints who had been tortured, killed, and burned at the stake. I was now ashamed to be Catholic.

Most Christians would say that the Sabbath is a Jewish day of worship and is not for the Christian. Not too long ago, I would have agreed with them. I grew up with the Catholic version of the Ten Commandments and always thought they were the ones God gave us. I would soon discover how incorrect I was and how the Catholic Church has tried to change God's law.

These changes are noted in *The Convert's Catechism of Catholic Doctrine*, stated in question/answer form:

Q. Which is the Sabbath day?
A. Saturday is the Sabbath day.

> Q. Why do we observe Sunday instead of Saturday?
>
> A. We observe Sunday instead of Saturday because the Catholic Church, in the Council of Laodicea (AD 336), transferred the solemnity from Saturday to Sunday.

So, I wondered, who gave the Catholic Church authority to change something that was "written with the finger of God" (see Exod. 31:18)?

According to a statement written by Lucius Ferraris in the article *Propta Bibliotheca,* Vol. VI, p. 29, "The Pope is of so great authority and power that he can modify, explain, or interpret even divine laws...The Pope can modify divine law, since his power is not of man, but of God, and he acts as vicegerent (representative) of God upon earth." Also, in the *Canon and Tradition*, p. 263 (of the Catholic Church): "The authority of the church could therefore not be bound to the authority of the Scriptures, because the Church had changed the Sabbath to Sunday, not by command of Christ, but by its own authority."

These changes to the commandments removed the second commandment that forbids idolatry (for obvious reasons) and divided the tenth commandment into two parts in order to retain a full ten-commandment law.

But wait, there was even more from the Book of Revelation that I would need to digest. "And on her forehead a name was written: MYSTERY, BABYLON THE GREAT, THE MOTHER OF HARLOTS AND OF THE ABOMINATIONS OF THE EARTH. I saw a woman, drunk with the blood of the saints and with the blood of the martyrs of Jesus. And when I saw her, I marveled with great amazement" (Rev. 17:5–6). It was explained that Babylon was the name symbolizing any religious organization that is confused in their teachings. The Lord confused the languages at the tower of Babel, and "Babel" is where we also get the word baby because a baby will babble when learning how to speak. The Mother Catholic Church is confused with her teachings. The harlots are the daughters of this church and are those how have spun off from her but still cling to some of her teachings, such as Sunday worship.

Even the colors spoken of in Revelation 17:4 indicate the Vatican as that great city: "The woman was arrayed in purple and scarlet, and adorned with gold." One cannot deny while looking at any one of the numerous pictures of the Vatican that the cardinals' vestments and the uniforms worn by the Papal Swiss guards are the same colors as those of the woman riding the beast of Revelation 17:4. These lessons were an extremely hard pill for me, a Catholic, to swallow. But how could I not? They came straight from the Bible and from history. These were not mere man's interpretations of what God may or may not have said. They were, in fact, God's written words.

So, there it was. Scripture, God's Word, all point to the Roman papacy as seated on the throne of the antichrist, and I was a member of that church. For sixty years, I had been led to believe I was worshipping in the true church, the one Protestants were supposed to come home to. How could I have been so deceived? "So then faith comes by hearing, and hearing by the word of God" (Rom. 10:17). Yes, I had heard. I had spent a large part of my adult life "hearing." Trouble was that the faith I had been hearing did not come from the Word of God. It came from the *Catechism of the Catholic Church*. For me, the one consolation in my early journey was knowing with all my heart that once I knew the Bible, once I knew Scripture for myself, it was going to point to the Catholic Church as the true church. And

I knew that I could then defend her. But that is not what happened. Instead, I grew to understand that the antichrist, the one books are written about and movies portray, oversaw the church I so loved.

In the weeks to follow, as I continued to attend Sunday Mass and perform the duties I had been hired years before to do, I began to feel like I was participating in a pagan ritual. I was becoming an "abomination," and my spirit was rebelling. I was not sure who I could turn to, knowing that without firsthand knowledge of what I was experiencing, no one I knew in the mother church was ever going to believe me. On the surface I was not sure it was true myself, but deep down, I did know because there it was. God's words written in black and white. It was here I came to realize I had been born in that great city. I had been born in Babylon.

I began to unravel even more. I did not know who to turn to or who to trust. I did not know what was real and what was not. My thoughts kept

> *It was here I came to realize I had been born in that great city. I had been born in Babylon.*

me up at night. My heart was screaming, "How could this be true!?" My dear, sweet husband was at a loss. He did not know how to comfort me, how to console the broken spirit in me. For months, I was an emotional, spiritual disaster. Finally, in his desperation to help me, my husband recommended I speak to a priest friend of mine. After all, I had known and trusted this man for many years and had worked side by side with him for most of that time. And so, I contacted Anthony*.

Chapter Five

Wrong Pasture

"And other sheep I have which are not of this fold; them also I must bring, and they will hear My voice; and there will be one flock and one shepherd" (John 10:16).

"Ignore it, Jane. These types of programs come out every now and then; it's nothing. Just ignore it." That was the answer I received from my Catholic priest friend in response to the session in the 2016

Unlock Revelation series titled "The Actual Unavoidable Identity of the Anti-Christ." I had forwarded some of the links of the videotaped meetings to him in an email and was looking for some answers, some guidance.

Anthony had been assigned to our parish. Because of my position as pastoral associate, we worked together on all aspects of parish life. He was a young priest with a very charismatic personality and could relate to just about anyone. We worked very well together, and he had even become my confessor. After he had been reassigned to another parish, we continued to remain friends. I knew he was someone I could trust. After all, he had been my shepherd, and Scripture tells me, "What man of you, having a hundred sheep, if he loses one of them, does not leave the ninety-nine in the wilderness, and go after the one which is lost until he finds it? And when he has found it, he lays it on his shoulders, rejoicing. And when he comes home, he calls together his friends and neighbors, saying to them, 'Rejoice with me, for I have found my sheep which was lost!'" (Luke 15:4–6).

I was in one of the darkest spiritual battles of my entire life, and I knew he was going to be able to explain all this to me and that I would find solace. Instead, he was telling me to *ignore* it! I honestly believe he could not have even taken the time to watch the video, or he would not be telling me this. Surely, he would have had some questions otherwise. My life was in an upheaval, and I was desperate for help! How could this man, this priest with whom I had worked for eight years, tell me to just ignore it? I was a lost sheep. Wasn't he a shepherd? I decided that it would do me no good to pursue any further conversation with him, and we had no more contact.

As I continued to go to church and perform my duties, light-bulb moments would present themselves. In Catholic tradition, August 15th commemorates the feast day of the Assumption of Mary and is considered a Holy Day of Obligation, in which Catholics are "obliged" to attend Mass for fear of committing a mortal sin. The belief is that Mary was "assumed" into heaven to be reunited with her soul instead of going through the natural process of physical decay upon death. I had believed this tradition up until my new understanding of the state of the dead, as taught in the *Unlock Revelation* series.

While attending Mass on this particular "holy day," the Scripture reading came from the Gospel of Luke and was only two verses long: "As Jesus was saying these things, a woman in the crowd called out, 'Blessed is the mother who gave you birth and nursed you.' He replied, 'Blessed rather are those who hear the word of God and obey it'" (Luke 11:27–28, NIV). As I followed along, using the missalette (liturgy guide), Jesus' own words, "Blessed *rather* are those who hear the word of God and obey it," struck a chord in me. My thoughts quickly said: *Doesn't anyone else hear what I am seeing and hearing? Jesus said "rather."*

Yes, I know we are to respect and love Mary for her willingness at such a young age to endure the embarrassment and shame that she experienced, to be the vessel that bore our Savior Jesus Christ. But to be "obliged" to attend Mass on this day now became ludicrous to me. More insights were to come.

One Sunday morning, while standing in the back of the church waiting for the bells to be rung and Mass to begin, our choir director was commenting on the upcoming 150th anniversary of the Marian apparition known as Our Lady of Fatima. The story is that Mary, the mother of Jesus, appeared to three small children in Portugal. Mary pleaded with the children to warn their people to keep saying the rosary. "If people will do what I tell you, many souls will be saved, and there will be peace."

As the choir director was walking away, Monsignor T.*, under his breath, made a very sarcastic remark. "Hah! Secret!" I was far enough along in my Protestant journey that my devotion to Mary had become nonexistent, and still, his comment kind of surprised me. What secret, and why is he being so flippant about it?

At home that afternoon, I pulled out my boxes of Catholic books and started digging. Two different copies of the Fatima story were among the bunch. *The Story of Fatima* and *The True Story of Fatima*. After watching a few of the *Unlock Revelation* videos, my approach to reading had changed. The fact that the word *true* was used in the title of one of these books made me wonder, is there a false story of Fatima?

What I found made me shake my head. The "secret" was written on the pages, plain as day, and would have been easily spotted by anyone with some Bible study background. But the average Catholic would never have found it. "2 Thess. 2:7" was printed among one of the sentences. "For the secret power of lawlessness is already at work; but the one who now holds it back will continue to do so til; he is taken out of the way."

Most Catholics do not read Scripture on their own. But I did, and one of the things I had learned was to never take Scripture out of context, so I read that passage to the very end: "And for this reason God will send them strong delusion, that they should believe the lie, that they all may be condemned who did not believe the truth but had pleasure in unrighteousness" (2 Thess. 2:11–12, NJKV).

> *Most Catholics do not read Scripture on their own. But I did, and one of the things I had learned was to never take Scripture out of context.*

According to *The True Story of Fatima,* "Pope Benedict XVI has stated that the Message of Fatima is the most ***prophetic message*** of the Twentieth Century." (page 4, paragraph 6, emphasis added). Prophetic? I asked myself what I had learned about prophecy at the *Unlock Revelation* seminars. All prophecy must lead us to God and not contradict the Bible.

Wrong Pasture 67

If prophecy needs to line up with God's written Word, does the "True Story" fit that definition? I began to read the entire book, not an easy task. It became an obsession. My level of anger constantly needed to be checked.

"Fear not! I am the Angel of Peace. Pray with me!" (page 5, paragraph 9). I had become a skeptic, and my thoughts instantly asked, who is this Angel of Peace? I took out my Bible app and searched "Angel of Peace" but came up empty. There is no Angel of Peace in the Bible. There is a Prince of Peace, Jesus Christ, but there is no angel of peace. This would be the first of many lies written in the pages of this "true story." The following excerpts are just a few examples contained in *The True Story of Fatima*.

Lucia asked some more questions of the Lady. Two girls who used to come to her house to learn sewing from her sisters had recently died. Lucia wanted to find out about them, too.

"And Maria do Rosario, daughter of Jose das Neves, is she in heaven?"

"*Yes*," the lady replied.

"And Amelia?"

"*She is still in purgatory.*"

According to Catholics, purgatory is the place where sinners go to be purified before they can enter heaven. Again, not found in God's Word. I was only on page fourteen, and there were eighty-two more pages to go. This was literally becoming a joke to me. How could I have ever believed such bald-faced lies? Of course, Catholics are not taught to read and study the Word of God; they are taught to obey, obey the nuns and the priests and the magisterium of the church. Another passage states:

"Frightened, deathly pale, the little ones raised their eyes to Our Lady for help as Lucia cried out. 'Oh…Our Lady!'

"Our Lady explained: **'You have seen Hell – where the souls of poor sinners go. To save them God wills to establish throughout the world the devotion to My Immaculate heart.**

"'If people will do what I tell you, many souls will be saved, and there will be peace.'"

As a child, I had been taught that hell is the place you go to if you are bad and don't confess your sins, a place where you will burn forever and ever. Scary thought for a child. What does Scripture say about death and hell?

Psalm 6:5: "For in death there is no remembrance of You; In the grave who will give You thanks?" Psalm 146:4: "His spirit departs, he returns to his earth; In that very day his plans perish." Ecclesiastes 9:5: "…the dead know nothing." Job 7:9: "…So he who goes down to the grave does not come up" (all NKJV). Scripture clearly defines the state of the dead. They go to their grave.

So, what about hell? According to Revelation 20:7–9, the satanic rebellion will be crushed. "Now when the thousand years have expired, Satan will be released from his prison and will go out to deceive the nations which are in the four corners of the earth, Gog and Magog, to gather them together to battle, whose number is as the sand of the sea. They went up on the breadth of the earth and surrounded the camp of the saints and the beloved city. And fire came down from God out of heaven and devoured them." Hell is not a place where you burn for eternity; it is an event.

Another phrase in the Marian literature: "To save them God wills to establish throughout the world the devotion to My [Mary's] Immaculate heart." I searched the biblical text and could not find any verses pertaining to devotion to Mary. What I did find was, "I am saying this for your own good, not to restrict you, but that you may live in a right way in *undivided devotion to the Lord*" (1 Cor. 7:35,

NIV, emphasis added). And "But I am afraid that just as Eve was deceived by the serpent's cunning, your minds may somehow be led astray from your *sincere and pure devotion to Christ"* (2 Cor. 11:3, NIV emphasis added).

Other "true story" quotes: "Her role as Mediatrix of All Graces." Again, we can see that this is totally contrary to sacred Scripture "For there is one God and one mediator between God and men, the Man Christ Jesus" (1 Tim. 2:5, NKJV).

I entered the word "grace" in one of my Bible app search engines, and according to the NIV, there are 113 places where the word appears. Almost every one of them pertains to God, Jesus Christ, or the Lord. My favorite is Ephesians 4:7: "But to each one of us grace has been given *as Christ apportioned it*." I would say that that settles who is the real "mediatrix of all graces." I was beginning to see a pattern.

The last quote disturbed me the most. It says: "And to continue praying the Rosary every day in honor of Our Lady of the Rosary, in order to obtain peace for the world and the end of the war, because *only She can help you* … July 13, 1917" (Page 95 listed under the heading *Words of Our Lady of Fatima*, emphasis added).

Only she can help you? I was shocked by this statement, and I believe that this one could be considered a blasphemy: "Because You, being a Man, make Yourself God" (John 10:33, NKJV).

I began to wonder if any Catholic had read the entire *The True Story of Fatima* and not seen the heresy. Has it always been there written so boldly? But then again, I *was* Catholic, and I had never read it! Now more scales began to fall from my eyes. No, they were being ripped off. And the truth, God's truth, was filling my heart, mind, and soul.

Performing my pastoral duties became more and more difficult. One of those duties was to prepare children who were at the age of accountability (generally around seven years old) for the sacrament of First Communion. To get myself prepared, I opened the teacher's manual of the children's version of the Catholic Catechism and began to read. False teachings seemed to pop up at me one by one.

In one of the lessons under the heading "Read From the Bible," in Lesson 1, pg. 12, it states: "Note: at the end of each lesson, readings will be suggested from the Bible. These are not given to prove the teachings of the catechism. We prove things from the teachings of the Church. The Bible was given by God to the Church to help in the explanations of its teachings." That seemed backward to me. According to 2 Timothy 3:16, "All Scripture is given by inspiration of God, and is profitable for doctrine, for reproof, for correction, for instruction in righteousness."

Another lesson came under the title "How To Make a Good Confession" (Lesson 32, pg. 203). These were in question-and-answer form. "Question: What should we do when we have committed no mortal sin since our last confession? Answer: When we have committed no mortal sin since our last confession, we should confess our venial sins and some sin told in a previous confession." If God forgives us of our sins and remembers them no more, why would there be a need to confess them over again? Matthew 18:6 helped me to start packing my bags for my journey out of Babylon, for it says: "Whoever causes one of these little ones who believe in Me to sin, it would be better for him if a millstone were hung around his neck, and he were drowned in the depth of the sea."

There was no way I was going to teach any child what was in these lessons. There was only one student that would have been making her First Communion. A year earlier, she had attended every preparation class with her older sister, and I was very confident that she was well informed. I contacted the parents and told them that according to the Catholic Church, she was ready for First Communion and that they would be responsible for any further studies with her. I just couldn't do it.

I began attending Mass less and less. I could barely stomach walking into the building, much less kneeling in prayer or participating in communion, drinking the "wine of her adulteries" (Rev. 14:8, NIV). I visited a few other Sunday-keeping churches, but the Sabbath, the seal of God, and the mark of the beast kept ringing in my ears. If I was going to leave Babylon, I needed to totally "get out of her." So, I began planning my exit. I wanted my departure to be virtually unnoticeable, as unnoticeable as it could possibly be. However, in my small church community, surely someone was going to notice that I was not there to participate in the ministries, as a lector, or to occupy my chair in the choir.

In October of 2016, I handed my letter of resignation to the Monsignor who was currently assigned to our parish. I did not inform him of my decision to leave the church. He was not an easy man to have a conversation with, and I was not spiritually strong enough for any kind of confrontation. He himself was getting ready to retire and understood that after nineteen years of service, I was ready to leave my position as pastoral associate. Because he was leaving his duties the following July, I indicated that I would stay on in a voluntary capacity to help with the transition of the new priest and with whoever would take over my position. I really was not sure exactly how that was all going to happen, considering I was having an exceedingly difficult time just walking into the church building. But still, I had made my commitment and felt obligated to it.

A few weeks after accepting my resignation, Monsignor noticed that I had not been attending Mass and questioned my sister about it, wondering if I was ill or something. She informed him that I was intending to leave the Catholic Church. His response was straight-forward: "Get my key," meaning the church key in my possession. My sister relayed his request to me through a text message. At first, I was devastated. How could he, my pastor, the shepherd of this flock, not even take the time to talk to me about my decision? I sat staring at my phone and started to cry. Another rejection from yet another Catholic priest.

And then, my shock turned into complete joy. The Almighty God, the God who had created the universe, had not forsaken me. This God had removed all responsibility from me! I no longer had to walk into the church that I had begun to loathe. Elation swelled up in me, and I began to praise God over and over again. I ran to my husband with tears of joy and relief. What a mighty God we serve! Without much hesitation, I removed my church key from my keychain and took it next door to my sister. "Go forth from Babylon! Flee from the Chaldeans! With a voice of singing, Declare, proclaim this, Utter it to the end of the earth; Say, 'The Lord has redeemed his servant Jacob'" (Isa. 48:20, NKJV). I was leaving Babylon quickly.

Some of my personal belongings were still there in the building. I made arrangements with my sister (who had her own key) to let me in to retrieve them. As she followed me around with a very watchful eye,

> *The Almighty God, the God who had created the universe, had not forsaken me. This God had removed all responsibility from me!*

I collected my things. Ezekiel's words were there for me, "By day you shall bring out your belongings in their sight, as though going into captivity; and at evening you shall go in their sight, like those who go into captivity" (Ezek. 12:4, NKJV). I was living proof of biblical truths and Ezekiel's prophecies. In fact, Ezekiel began to speak powerfully to me.

Chapter Six

Ezekiel's Role

"And He said to me, 'Son of man, stand on your feet, and I will speak to you.'" (Ezek. 2:1)

And speak He did. As more and more biblical truths were being revealed to me through the *Unlock Revelation* seminar, the books of Daniel and Revelation led to the writings of Ezekiel. A divine appointment, maybe? All I know is that I continued to devour his text, which seemed to parallel my life and soon began to convict me of many things. A huge conviction pertained to the Catholic "sacramentals" that were present in almost every room of my home. "They took pride in their beautiful jewelry and used it to make their detestable idols. They made it into vile images; therefore I will make it a thing unclean for them" (Ezekiel 7:20, NIV). Inside and out, pictures, statues, and many other works of art depicting God, Jesus, Mary, saints, and angels covered the walls, sat on tables, and adorned my gardens. I had been adding these "vile images" to my home for my whole life. Babylon is **very** pretty.

I had rosaries, lots of them, rosaries of various sizes, colors, kinds, and quality. I even had rosaries from other countries purchased for me as gifts from one of my sons as he traveled the world serving this country. Now when I think of a rosary, Revelation 17:4 resonates in my mind. "The woman was arrayed in purple and scarlet, and adorned with gold, precious stones, and **pearls** ..."

"But thus you shall deal with them: you shall destroy their altars, and break down their sacred pillars, and cut down their wooden images, and burn their carved images with fire" (Deut. 7:5, NKJV). I could not remove the "idols" from my home fast enough. These abominations needed to go, and they needed to go now. I began removing pictures from the walls and slicing them up with a knife. If they had glass, the glass was smashed with a hammer, and beautiful frames were broken. Rosary beads were cut up and the "pearls" tossed in the trash. "...you shall not covet the silver or gold that is on them, nor take it for yourselves, lest you be snared by it; for it is an abomination to the Lord your God" (Deuteronomy 7:25).

An incredibly beautiful concrete statue of Mary, Jesus' mother, which I had placed in a garden close to the main entrance to our home, probably took the brunt of my anger. "And to my dismay, women were sitting there weeping for Tammuz" (Ezek. 8:14, NKJV). One of the slides presented during the *Unlock Revelation* seminar was a picture of Tammuz, which took on an eerie likeness to Mary holding the child Jesus in her arms. Now, all I could see as I looked at my statue was a pagan goddess welcoming visitors into my home.

This statue was fairly new, solid, and very heavy, too heavy for me to lift by myself. And I was in no mood to wait for help. With many smashes of my hammer, another graven image was gone. "Nor shall you bring an abomination into your house, lest you be doomed to destruction like it. You shall utterly detest it and utterly abhor it, for it is an accursed thing" (Deut. 7:26, NKJV).

My stomach ached, and I wanted to throw up. I was so angry. "They will loathe themselves for the evils which they committed in all their abominations" (Ezek. 6:9, NKJV). Sixty years of Satan's lies made visible in these things were now a pile of broken glass, chunks of cement, and shredded canvas, waiting for the garbage truck to pick it up. Trash day could not arrive fast enough, and I did not care who saw the pile sitting on the edge of my yard. I was done being Catholic, I was done living in Babylon, and I needed to completely "come out of her."

In the meantime, Ezekiel wasn't stopping there, and as long as he had my attention, he had a lot more to say. "Then He said to me: 'Son of man, go to the people of Israel and speak My words to them. You are not sent to a people of unfamiliar speech and hard language, but to the house of Israel" (Ezek. 3:4–5, NKJV).

I needed to go to my family, my big Catholic family, and speak His words to them. These are my people; they know me, and I need to warn them. Surely, they will listen to what I have to say. They needed to experience what I had experienced through *Unlock Revelation*. They needed to see how "Precept must be upon precept, precept upon precept, Line upon line, line upon line, Here a little, there a little" (Isa. 28:10 NKJV) would explain with great clarity exactly what the God of the Bible was expecting of us as true followers of His Son, Jesus Christ. I know I am not qualified to be the spokesperson of theological truths, but I felt I must still try because Ezekiel literally scared me. "When I say to a wicked person, 'You will surely die,' and you do not warn them or speak out to dissuade them from their evil ways in order to save their life, that wicked person will die for their sin, and *I will hold you accountable for their blood*" (Ezek. 3:18, NIV).

I decided to go to my older sister first. She and I were very close, and we always did the "churchy" stuff together. Even though she had lived in another state, often we would go on church retreats, attend lectures, visit shrines of Mary, and, of course, recite the rosary together. When my elderly mother, who lived next door to me, made the decision to move into an independent living facility, she deeded the house over to my sister and her husband. After their retirement, they moved in. She and I were both excited about the move because now we could become prayer partners and continue to grow in our faith together. Ezekiel came along for that visit: "And he said to me, 'Son of man, listen carefully and take to heart all the words I speak to you. Go now to your people in exile and speak to them. Say to them, 'This is what the Sovereign Lord says,' whether they listen or fail to listen" (Ezek. 3:10–11, NIV).

As I sat in her home, trying to explain what I was learning, I could sense that my warnings were falling on deaf ears. It soon became evident that there was no way she was going to believe that her "true church" was in any way, shape, or form in association with the antichrist. How could I blame her? If it had not been for a one-page handbill delivered to the "current resident" announcing the *Unlock Revelation* seminar, neither would I have believed. My sister was not going to listen to me, and she certainly was not going to participate in any teachings that weren't Catholic. I knew asking her to spend the time to watch twenty-one one-hour videos on Revelation's prophecies was clearly out of the question. She even voiced her concern that I was "under attack by Satan to leave the Catholic Church." I couldn't help but think, doesn't she realize that Satan rules this world, and we are all constantly "under attack?" If only she would listen to the TRUTH. How can I make her realize that God is warning us to "get out of her, My people" and that the enemy is probably very unhappy that I'm leaving the Catholic Church, for I know the truth, and that truth really does make you free? I left my sister's house with a very heavy heart.

Ezekiel's Role

Was this really happening? How could all this be so real? I felt, and still do, that I was living in a different realm. The Bible was no longer this obscure book with stories of prophets of long ago and spiritual beings far from my grasp. As I continued my journey with Ezekiel, these words were now living large and in my face.

I dared not reach out to my mother at this time, for I knew she was going to be even more difficult to talk to. Distance is what I needed to gain new strength, and so for a few months, I did not speak to any members of my family.

> *Distance is what I needed to gain new strength.*

Chapter Seven

Mary, Queen of Heaven?

"Who exchanged the truth about God for the lie, and worshiped and served the creature rather than the Creator, who is forever praised. Amen." Rom. 1:25

In the Catholic tradition, Mary, the mother of Jesus, is the Queen of Heaven. She also comes under many other titles: Our Lady of Fatima, Our Lady of Guadeloupe,

Mary, Queen of Heaven?

Our Lady of Medjugorje, and the Mediatrix of all graces, just to name a few. The Catholic Church I attended and where I received most of the sacraments was even named after Mary, Our Lady of Perpetual Help. A large statue of her adorned the sanctuary, and an even bigger icon hanging on the back wall greeted you as you exited the main body of the church. From childhood, I was saturated in Marian devotions. So biblically, where does Mary belong?

As my research of Mary continued, my exit out of Babylon became a reality. My mother had a hard time accepting my decision, and communication with her was almost non-existent. I still needed to try to explain to her my findings. Mom has a very strong devotion to "Our Lady," and I felt the need to warn her concerning biblical truths. I knew this was not going to be an easy task, but if I did not say something, I knew I would be held "accountable for their blood" (Ezek. 3:20, NKJV).

I finally made arrangements for a visit with Mom and went prepared with my Bible and a copy of *The True Story of Fatima,* with "blasphemies" highlighted. Surely, once she read it for herself, she would start to understand, and hopefully, the scales would begin to fall from her eyes. Unfortunately, this meeting did not go well. Each time I used the word "Bible," she would utter a combination of a giggle and a "hah!," and with every subsequent mention of the word, her utterance became louder and more intense. It scared me, and I began to wonder what other forces were in that apartment with us.

When I brought out the "True Story," she would not even look at it. "I'm not reading your stuff!" is what she exclaimed. "Mom, this is your stuff," I replied in dismay. I asked her if she had read it. "Yes," was her reply. So, I asked her if she understood what all it said, and again her reply was an emphatic "Yes." Later, in a subsequent conversation with my mother and one of my sisters, she accused me of slamming the book down on her coffee table with such force as to rip the cover page off. I had to remind her that it was already ripped when I brought it there, probably from my intense reading of it prior to the visit.

I also tried to explain, concerning reciting the rosary and bowing to her statue of Mary, that Scripture says: "And when you pray, do not use vain repetitions as the heathen do. For they think they will be heard for their many words" (Matt. 6:7, NKJV). My words fell on deaf ears. So many times, she had told me that the rosary "brings us closer to Jesus." And yet, during the same conversation, Mom stated that some nights as she lay in bed, she wondered why Jesus didn't speak to her. My heart and mind were screaming, "Put down the rosary, pick up a Bible, and He will talk to you!"

This incident indicated to me that Catholic traditions carry more weight than the truth of God's very own words. Jesus confronted Pharisees and teachers in Matthew, saying, "Thus you have made the commandment of God of no effect by your tradition. Hypocrites! Well did Isaiah prophesy about you, saying: 'These people draw near to Me with their mouth, And honor Me with their lips, But their heart is far from Me. And in vain they worship Me, Teaching as doctrines the commandments of men'" (Matt. 15:6–9).

Ellen G. White's commentary on Matthew 15 explains why such hypocrisy exists. She writes: "Satan has wrought with deceiving power, bringing in a multiplicity of errors that obscure truth. Error could not stand alone, and would soon become extinct if it did not fasten itself like a parasite upon the tree of truth. Error draws its life from the truth of God. The traditions of men, like floating germs, attach themselves to the truth of God, and men regard them as a part of the truth. Through false doctrines Satan gains a foothold, and captivates the minds of men, causing them to hold theories that have no foundation in truth. Men boldly teach for doctrines the commandments of men, and as traditions pass on from age to age, they acquire a power over the human mind. But age does not make error truth, neither does its burdensome weight cause the plant of truth to become a parasite. The tree of truth bears its own genuine fruit, showing its true origin and nature. The parasite of error also bears its own fruit, and makes manifest that its character is diverse from the plant of heavenly origin" (Letter 43, 1895, par. 41).

I left my meeting with Mom feeling very discouraged. I needed to step back from any further conversations concerning the mother of our Lord and pray that seeds of truth had not landed on rocky ground. Mom does read the Bible, but without spiritual guidance, the true meaning of the written Word makes little sense. In my experience, there are no adequate teachers of His Word in the Catholic Church.

So, biblically, who is the Queen of Heaven then? She is mentioned in the Bible, but only in the book of Jeremiah. "The children gather wood, the fathers kindle the fire, and the women knead dough, to make cakes for the queen of heaven; and they pour out drink offerings to other gods, that they may provoke Me to anger" (Jer. 7:18). I grew up believing that the "Queen of Heaven" was Mary, the mother of our Lord, because that is what I was told. Through God's holy Word, I came to realize that my new faith was coming through the hearing of Christ's voice in that Word.

Our Lady of Fatima, Our Lady of Lourdes, Our Lady of Guadalupe, Our Lady of Medjugorje, Our Lady of Good Hope, Our Lady of Perpetual Help, and so many more merely come from the father of lies! "And no wonder! For Satan himself transforms himself into an angel of light" (2 Cor. 11:14, NKJV). There is no one on earth who will ever be able to convince me that these Marian apparitions are none other than Satan in disguise.

Many devout Catholics will tell you that they do not worship Mary, that they honor her. I heard that statement throughout my entire life. But when I look at the numerous pictures of people gathering to "honor" Mary, I see those people kneeling in adoration, forgetting the commandment that says: "You shall not bow down to them" (Deut. 5:9, NKJV).

> *I knew what door was being opened for me, and I knew it was time to walk through it.*

Alexander Graham Bell is quoted as saying: "When one door closes another one opens; but we so often look so long and so regretfully upon the closed door that we do not see the ones which open for us." It was now time for me to close the Catholic door and not look back. I knew what door was being opened for me, and I knew it was time to walk through it.

Chapter Eight

Becoming Adventist

"He who overcomes shall be clothed in white garments, and I will not blot out his name from the Book of Life; but I will confess his name before My Father and before His angels" (Rev. 3:5)

In November of 2017, my journey as an Adventist began when I walked through the front doors of the Marquette Seventh-day Adventist Church. It had been almost a year and a half after attending the first session of the *Unlock Revelation* seminar. I was alone and extremely nervous. The only Adventist I knew was Pastor Aron Crews, and I had not actually met him in person. I had watched the seminar videos so many times and knew that voice so well that I felt like he was an old friend. Unfortunately, I would soon learn that he was no longer the pastor in Marquette, as he had been reassigned to a church in another part of our state.

When I walked into the church for the first time, I was met by Jeff. Jeff wasn't the greeter; he just happened to be the first person I saw as I entered the foyer. He had the biggest smile on his face and was so welcoming that I felt like I was home. To my amazement, there were children running down the hallway of the church. It was noisy, and I loved it! Jeff pointed me to the sanctuary and let me know that worship was beginning in a few minutes. I was not sure what to expect, but so far, it felt right.

I was not disappointed. Worship started off with a song service. It appeared that everyone was joining in on all the wonderful hymns, not something I was used to in my former church. Services continued with an elder standing up and asking if there were any prayer requests. Church members began speaking right there from their seats! This never would have happened in my Catholic Church. There, prayers of petition would have been taken from an authorized "Book of Prayers," and any special prayer requests required a $10 contribution. This way of petitioning for prayer was foreign to me, but I really liked it.

Next came the Little Lambs' offering. As the pianist played music, children began to congregate toward the front of the church, where they were handed little baskets. They carried these through the congregation while members placed pocket change into them. Once the baskets were returned to the altar, it was time for the children's story. I sat in amazement and kept thinking: *this is so cool*. I hadn't seen this many kids in church in a very long time, and here, they were actually part of the worship service.

More songs followed, and then, the main offering was taken. Next, the pastor stood up front and began preaching. I do not recall what the sermon was on that particular Sabbath, but I do remember that we were told to turn to this verse and then to that verse in our Bibles. Once again, I had not brought a Bible. It is not what Catholics do. I was amazed at how many different Scripture passages were used during one sermon. And we were expected to look each one up along with the preacher and follow what was read. I noticed that under each seat was a Bible, so I picked one up and tried to follow along. With my limited knowledge of where to find each book and chapter, I decided to just sit back and absorb everything that was being said. This was all new to me, and what really surprised me was that the pastor spoke for forty-five minutes! I was not prepared for this, but most assuredly, was delighted. I was so hungry when I had walked into that building and was so full when I left. Yes, I was home.

I think we all know that in a smaller congregation, if there is a visitor, everyone notices! When worship ended, I was greeted by some of the women from the church. They were, of course, curious as to who this stranger was and how I had come to the Adventist church. I was pleased to tell them that over a year ago, I had attended an *Unlock Revelation* seminar and that my journey had brought me there. This is when I met my dear friend Carol.

Carol called me a few days later and asked if we could meet. She even welcomed me to her home. I wasn't too sure about that and suggested we meet at a local restaurant, which we did. Our first meeting was such a joy. We talked like we were sisters, and the time just flew by. I couldn't wait to become a part of this church family.

I had not been attending my "new" church very long, maybe just a few weeks, when I informed some of my new church family that I wanted to be baptized and that I did not want to wait. Little did they know that for years I had felt cheated out of this important step. I had been baptized by sprinkling as an infant but had no recollection of it. During some of my former studies, I had learned that baptism should be done by immersion, and so here I was, fourteen years later, making that very important decision for myself. I wanted to shout it from the mountain top and let the whole world know that it was my decision to be a follower of Jesus Christ.

Another wish that I had at that time was that Pastor Aron Crews be the one to baptize me. After all, he was the one I had come to love and respect through his teaching in *Unlock Revelation*. His was the voice I had come to know. He was the one who had led me out of the lies of Babylon into the truth of the gospel, and he was the one who I wanted to take me from certain death to rebirth.

Knowing that Pastor Crews had been assigned to another church in a different part of the state of Michigan, I wondered if this was even possible. I figured all I could do was ask. Several times during the course of the seminar, he had mentioned that if we ever had any questions, we were free to contact him. He let us know that he was eager to make sure that we had the answers we were looking for. Our knowledge of God's truth was his passion, and he wasn't hesitant to give out his cell phone number. Keep in mind that it had now been a year and a half since *Unlock Revelation* had been presented, and it is not uncommon for cell phone numbers to change rather quickly. I did not know if he would even receive my message. I decided to be bold and give it a try, so I sent him a text and prayed he would receive it.

You will never know the excitement I felt when not twenty minutes after hitting that "send" button, my phone started to ring. I had entered his contact information into my phone, so I could see on my caller ID that it was Pastor Aron Crews who was calling me back. I froze. First of all, because I was in shock that he was calling back so quickly, but also because where I live, cell reception isn't always reliable. My fear was that we would lose the connection as soon as I answered his call.

I stood as still as I could and hit the green answer button. "Please, Lord, don't let this call hang up" was my immediate prayer.

"Hello, Jane, this is Pastor Aron Crews."

"Yes, I know, and if this call disconnects, I will call you back from my landline," spewed out of my mouth. At least now, my bases were covered, and I could relax a little.

God is so very good. My twenty-minute conversation with Pastor Crews did not disconnect. He was full of questions, and I was more than happy to tell him my story. I boldly asked him to come back to Marquette to baptize me and even more boldly requested a particular Sabbath. I wanted to be baptized on January 27, 2018, the day after my earthly birthday. And I wanted my rebirth to coincide with it.

I realized that he would have to speak to those in authority to get permission for this

> *"Please, Lord, don't let this call hang up"*

to happen. He assured me he would do his best and was pleased to be included in this special day.

This conversation took place in early November, giving us two months to plan the event. Even if he could not make it, I was going to get baptized! Fortunately, my prayers were answered very quickly, and permission was given for him to come to Marquette on that Sabbath. We only had one more hurdle to jump. The Marquette Church had no baptistry.

If you've ever been to Michigan's Upper Peninsula in the month of January, you know that our lakes and rivers are mostly frozen over. Even the Great Lakes' crown jewel, Lake Superior, located only a few miles from the church, would not make for a proper baptism for my aging body. I did not wish to visit an Adventist Church forty miles away, which had a baptistry, because I had come to love my new home and wanted as many of my new brothers and sisters in Christ to be present. So, I did the next best thing. I asked the church board for permission to build my own baptismal tank. I was very pleased that without any hesitation, they said "yes." Now, I needed to come up with a plan.

I am a person who loves crafts. I am also blessed to work part-time for a nonprofit organization that sells donated, used building supplies. The Marquette County Habitat for Humanity ReStore would have everything I needed for the project. It just so happened that in the fenced-in storage yard outdoors, there was a large corner bathtub which would be perfect for the occasion. After explaining to my manager, who happens to be an elder at a Sunday-keeping church, what it would be used for, he agreed to sell it to me at a very reduced price.

Although the tub was large, it was not as deep as it should be for a full immersion. Not wanting to leave any room for a baptismal faux pas, I decided that the walls of the tub needed to be extended upward to accommodate the proper amount of water. All needed supplies were purchased, and construction could soon begin ... but where? This was a huge undertaking, and logistically, the best place would be at the church itself. Again, to my pleasant surprise, the church board agreed without hesitation to let me build my own baptistry in the sanctuary of our church.

At the beginning of January, construction began, giving us only three weeks to finish the project. With the help of my husband, Dan, and my former therapist, now friend, Tom, we were able to raise the sides with a wooden frame, cover it with ceramic tile, and make everything waterproof. Finishing touches were added to the background, which made it look like it was part of the sanctuary. My dream for baptism was becoming a reality.

During the months leading up to this day, I was not only a carpenter; I was also being prepared spiritually. I devoured the lessons on the *28 Fundamental Beliefs of the Church* with delight. I was so hungry. I wanted to make sure to taste every morsel that was offered. I had been looking forward to this day for so long, and I didn't want to miss out on anything. When that day arrived, I wanted to be ready.

The night before my baptism, Pastor Crews and Carol met me at the church to go over my decision. Remember, up to this point, I hadn't even officially met Pastor Crews in person, and this would give us an opportunity to get to know each other a little beforehand. As I waited at the church for them to arrive, I was arranging some last-minute details on the baptistry when I heard Pastor Crews come into the church. Others were there, and as he stopped to greet them, my thoughts shouted, "That's the voice I know!" My heart was overjoyed to finally meet the person who brought me to Christ. Tears still come when I think of that day.

We sat and talked for about an hour, going over the beliefs of the church, commitments I would be making, what baptism really means, and a few other details concerning the logistics of the ceremony. It was such a delight to speak to Pastor Crews in person, and I could not wait for my new life as a disciple to begin.

During our conversation, the topic of jewelry came up, and Pastor Crews mentioned the three black bands on my wrists. I explained that they were not really jewelry and that they had very symbolic meaning for me. Each one reminded me of three of the demons (alcohol, depression, and anxiety) that Jesus had conquered in my life. I adamantly told Pastor Crews that they would never come off my wrists (or so I thought) and that I would go to my grave with them on. He accepted my reasoning and graciously dropped the subject. God would make His will on this matter very plain to me later.

The next morning, during Sabbath worship, Pastor Crews baptized me in the baptistry that Dan, Tom, and I had built. The actual baptism only took a few seconds, but those seconds will stay with me forever. One of the most vivid feelings I experienced was while being submerged. Even though the water was just inches deep, I felt like I was plunged many feet down, and the sound of water rushing past my ears was surreal. As Pastor Crews lifted my head above the water, I indeed felt as if I had been pulled out of the depths and brought into a new life. On that day, January 27, 2018, a new baby Christian was born. On that day, the remnant Seventh-day Adventist Church gained a new baby sister in Christ, and her name is Jane.

Epilogue

Life as An Adventist — A New Beginning

"Cast away from you all the transgressions which you have committed, and get yourselves a new heart and a new spirit. For why should you die, O house of Israel?" (Ezek. 18:31)

As I began my new life as an Adventist, I felt such a peace in my heart, a peace I would not be able to explain. That peace would be needed in the days to follow, as my family had a hard time accepting my decision to leave the Catholic Church. Very soon, I found a Scripture verse that would be my saving grace in this situation, and I continue to keep it very close to my heart. "So Jesus answered and said, 'Assuredly, I say to you, there is no one who has left house or brothers or sisters or father or mother or wife or children or lands, for My sake and the gospel's, who shall not receive a hundredfold now in this time—houses and brothers and sisters and mothers and children and lands, with persecutions—and in the age to come, eternal life" (Mark 10:29–30, NKJV).

As I continued my spiritual journey with Jesus, my relationship with my own family was becoming non-existent. I was living out Mark 10:29–30 in a very personal way, but I knew God would not forsake me. And so, I kept my eyes on Him and committed myself to moving forward, excited to see what He had in store for me. Who would these new "brothers and sisters" be? What would these new "lands" look like? How would I be blessed "a hundredfold"? It did not take me long to discover how rich my life was about to become and how God holds true to His promises.

Very soon after my baptism, my new sister in Christ, Carol, gifted me with a study guide titled *The Discipleship Handbook*. I had come to love and appreciate Carol and looked forward to our weekly meetings with this book. Each week, I grew and learned so much about becoming an Adventist. Those sessions also taught me the importance of a person's testimony. In the Catholic Church, witnessing is not something you hear from the pulpit. The first time I was asked to stand up and give my testimony at my new church, I was thrilled and excited. Here was an opportunity to let others know exactly how it came to be that this cradle Catholic would find herself in a Sabbath-keeping church.

While attending my first local camp meeting with my husband, I was sitting in the audience when the speaker announced that they were going to pass the microphone around and that if the Spirit so moved, anyone could witness about how God was working in their life. As the usher with the mic approached my section, my heart started beating, and I could feel a panic attack building up inside of me. This audience was much bigger than my small local church, and Satan whispered, "You can't do this. What makes you think you can stand up and tell your story. Nobody cares." I knew this was not of God. As the usher came to my row of chairs, I stood. My voice was shaking at first, but as I continued to speak, my panic attack subsided, and my speech calmed down. When I finished, I heard a huge "AMEN" from the crowd. All I could think was, *Thank You, Lord, for being there with me and getting me through this.*

Afterward, many people approached and thanked me for my story. It was then that

I knew that with the help of the Holy Spirit, I could do just about anything. This moment was the highlight of the weekend for me. Nothing else could possibly beat this mountaintop experience. How was I to know that this would not compare to other experiences God had planned for me?

> *It was then that I knew that with the help of the Holy Spirit, I could do just about anything.*

On the two-hour drive home, my thoughts were on the events of the weekend when the black bands that I wore on my wrists began to feel very heavy. That seemed odd because my hands were resting on my lap, and I could not figure out why they would feel so heavy. Then suddenly, very clearly, I heard a voice in my head saying, "Take them off!" It startled me, and I froze. "Take them off!" now repeated sternly. It scared me, and I quickly took them off my wrists. Immediately after removing the black bands, the voice spoke again, very gently, "I have other things for you to focus on." Never had I experienced something so profound in my life. And true to the voice, I have found many other things to focus on since then.

I became active in my local church in the joy of service. Those "lands" included becoming a deaconess, adult Sabbath School teacher, joining a small choir, and leading out in the song service as a chorister, to name a few. Many doors opened for me to give my testimony, some of those testimony times being live-streamed into 130 different countries. I volunteered at Historic Adventist Village for a week, dressing in period clothing and meeting so many wonderful people. Vespers talks, a podcast, and now a book!

Not only was God placing me in service to His church, but He was also gently convicting me of those areas in my life that were not healthy. Soon, I gave up caffeine and started a vegetarian lifestyle. And then the greatest testimony of His healing power; my marijuana use.

After hearing a brief health talk on how marijuana affects the frontal lobe of the brain, I experienced the biggest conviction up to this point. I liked how marijuana made me feel, and I certainly had no plans on giving it up. I literally cried out loud to God and told Him if He wanted me to stop using it, He was going to have to remove the urge because I was not quitting. Two days later, while standing outside,

I opened my little plastic bag of marijuana, turned it inside out, and let the contents blow into the wind. The urge has never returned.

It amazes me how God can orchestrate events in our lives to place you in situations that allow you to be a witness of His saving grace to others. You see, my husband's journey was also on the move.

Up to this point, Dan, who had always been so incredibly supportive of my journey, was now being awakened by the Holy Spirit. He started attending church with me and soon was sitting next to me during Sabbath School. He even watched the twenty-one videos of the revised *Unlock Revelation* seminars. In late February of 2020, Dan surprised me one day as he entered my prayer room unexpectedly and announced: "I need to get baptized—now!" Three weeks later, my dear, sweet husband was baptized in a hot tub at the home of church members. I do not know who was happier at that baptism, my husband or myself. Our journeys have now converged on the same path with the Holy Spirit as our guide, our focus on Jesus, and heaven as our destination. Our marriage is stronger than it has ever been. We have been pulled out of the miry pits of alcohol, drugs, tobacco, depression, and

Life as An Adventist — A New Beginning

anxiety. Gone are the days of me listening to my programs alone in my prayer room. Our journey as husband and wife has reminded us of where we were without God and where we are today ... saved by His grace!

Bibliography

Amazing Discoveries. "The Pope Claims to be God on Earth." https://1ref.us/1q7 (accessed October 13, 2021).

Deharbe, Joseph. *A Complete Catechism of the Catholic Religion (1847)*. Los Angeles: HardPress Publishing, 2013.

De Marchi, Fr. John. *The True Story of Fatima*. KIC, 2015. Kindle Edition.

"Did the Catholic Church Change the 10 Commandments?" The Apple of God's Eye, March 31, 2009. https://1ref.us/1q8 (accessed October 13, 2021).

Ferraris, F. Lucii. *Propta Bibliotheca, Canonica, Juridica, Moralis, Theologica, nec non Ascetica, Polemica, Rubricistica, Historica*, Vol. VI. Paris: J. P. Migne, 1860.

Great Encyclical Letters of Leo XIII. New York: Benziger Brothers, 1903. https://1ref.us/1ai (accessed August 19, 2021).

The Convert's Catechism of Catholic Doctrine. St. Louis, MO: B. Herder Book Company, 1910.

Lecky, W.E.H. *History of the Rise and Influence of the Spirit of Rationalism in Europe,* vol. 2, Revised edition. New York: D. Appleton, 1919.

Lette, Joshua. "The King of this World." *Lines and Precepts,* 2016. https://1ref.us/1q0 (accessed August 19, 2021).

Liguori, Alphonsus. *Dignities and Duties of the Priest*, vol. 12 (1887). CreateSpace Independent Publishing Platform, 2015.

Ministerial Association of the General Conference of Seventh-day Adventists. *Seventh-day Adventists Believe*. Hagerstown, MD: Review and Herald Publishing Association, 1988.

Pope Pius IX, *Cum Catholica Ecclesia*, March 26, 1860. https://1ref.us/1q1 (accessed August 19, 2021).

Rickaby, Reverend Joseph. *The Modern Papacy*, in *Lectures on the History of Religions*, Vol. 3, Lecture 24. London: Catholic Truth Society, 1910.

Schaff, Philip. *The History of the Christian Church,* Vol. 3. Grand Rapids, MI: Christian Classics Ethereal Library,1882.

Strong, James. *Strong's Exhaustive Concordance*. Peabody, MA; Hendrickson Publishing, 2009.

"Roman Catholic Ten Commandments." The Ten Commandments. https://1ref.us/1q3 (accessed August 19, 2021).

Veith, Walter. *Truth Matters: Escaping the Labyrinth of Error*. British Columbia: Amazing Discoveries, 2002.

TEACH Services, Inc.
P U B L I S H I N G

We invite you to view the complete
selection of titles we publish at:
www.TEACHServices.com

We encourage you to write us
with your thoughts about this,
or any other book we publish at:
info@TEACHServices.com

TEACH Services' titles may be purchased in
bulk quantities for educational, fund-raising,
business, or promotional use.
bulksales@TEACHServices.com

Finally, if you are interested in seeing
your own book in print, please contact us at:
publishing@TEACHServices.com

We are happy to review your manuscript at no charge.

www.ingramcontent.com/pod-product-compliance
Lightning Source LLC
Chambersburg PA
CBHW070544170426
43200CB00011B/2542